I0082106

Mobilize your Action Plan

(M.A.P)

A Realistic Guide for
ACHIEVING YOUR GOAL

Written By

DAVID E. BROWN, SR

Forwarded By Pastor James E. Wright

ON *Eighty* LEADER I BOOKS

© 2012 by David Brown Published by Oneighty Books 5577 University Ave San Diego, CA 92105 www.oneightyleader.com

ISBN 978-0-9854609-0-7

Printed in the United States of America

Contents

Acknowledgements

I'm thankful for the Lord Jesus Christ for dying on Calvary cross for my sins over 2000 years ago. Jesus Grace and Mercy is the only reason that I can write this book, expressing the power to create your reality through Christ. I'm also thankful for my lovely wife Jessica Lynn Brown and my son David Brown, Jr.

I'm also thankful for my father-in-law Pastor James Wright and mother-in-law Shelia Wright for being great parents and great leaders in my local church New Ark of the Covenant Church. Thanks for your sacrifices during my book writing.

Thank your grandma Bettie Eubank for taking me in as a child and pushing me to become my best. Mom I thank you for bring me in this world and your special motherly love.

Thanks: Taj Fuller, Angelia Fuller, Tiffany Fowler, Marquise Fowler, Rene Echo's, Michael Echo's, Michael Blue, Jeneen Blue, to all of the young people that I pastor, and many more…

Forward

You can find many supervisors, managers, bishops, pastors, and even presidents, but very few leaders. When I think of great leaders I'm reminded of people like President George Washington, President Abraham Lincoln, Moses, King David, Steve Jobs, Michael Jordan, Martin Luther King, Bishop T.D. Jakes, Bishop Paul Morton, Pastor Rick Warren, Bishop Henry Alexander, and many others. There are certain criteria that I believe makes a great leader like: God Fearing, Courage, Unselfish Love, Integrity, and Courage. As you read this book that my son has written to help empower the kingdom of God, please consider how there is an eagle inside of you that is ready to live, you just have to set it free. My church has been through this program and I believe that its life changing simply because we need more great leaders in our churches, in congress, business and the world at large.

Today I challenge you to dedicate and commit yourself to the leader in you, be strong and the Lord in the power of His might. It's possible for you to be successful, just keep Jesus as the center of your life. The Lord has blessed me to own several companies, which sold for hundreds of thousands of dollars, but I always kept him first. Now my son has taken this legacy of providing an underground railroad to free the mind of leaders who have become slaves to failure and regret. It stops today, discover your purpose, find your passion, and LEAD LET'S GO.

James Wright

**Senior Pastor & Founder of
New Ark Church, San Diego, CA**

Preface

Hello friend. I may not know you personally, but I know about you. I know that you want to do something about your life. Your dreams are reachable, your ideas are attainable, and your aspirations are significant. This book is geared to help make your goals a reality.

THE 80/20 RULE

The value of the Pareto Principle for a manager or leader is that it reminds you to focus on the 20 percent that matters. Of the things you do during your day, only 20 percent really matter. Those 20 percent produce 80 percent of your results. Identify and focus on those things. When the fire drills of the day begin to sap your time, remind yourself of the 20 percent you need to focus on. If something in the schedule has to slip, if something isn't going to get done, make sure it's not part of that 20 percent.

TAKE ACTION, YOUR LIFE COUNTS ON IT!

Your life is too valuable for you to waste time continuing to do anything to change the course of your life. Don't leave this world with regret and hopes of what you wish you could have done. The richest place in the world is the graveyard. Don't take your ideas and needed leadership to the grave, take a step into change now!

Introduction

Four years ago I was placed on orders to Augusta, Georgia by the United States Army to attend training school. After being in school for about two weeks I started a small Bible Study that started with 10 soldiers and then grew to 50 soldiers in about two weeks. I was teaching a lesson talking about faith in the book of Hebrews. I asked a question to these soldiers (ages ranged from 18-35) what is your plan of action for your life? Only 3 of them could answer my question, and the most common answer was I'd just wait and see. The issue I saw with this was that the average number of Christians in this study was 40 out of 50 and majority had been in church for at least 5 years. Here I began to understand the scripture that tells us that, "faith without works is dead." After this bible study I remember going back to my room crying out before God, because I felt that there was a need for a program that could help Christians create a plan of actions for their life. Today 7 out of every 10 people in a my survey said that they would write a grocery list to go to the store, but only 3 out of every 10 people said that they would write out daily goals, weekly goals, or yearly goals. The average person that writes a New Year's resolution normally will give it up in 30 days or less.

It was this research that caused me to seek God about a solution that revolutionizes Christians master their goals and achieve them. This caused me to introduce a program called Action Plan the Movement. All 50 of these Christians joined this six-week program to help them create realistic goals and produce great results. First thing that happened 20 of those who been awaiting a board to promote actual made rank. Secondly, our group grew from 50 to 175 members within 7 weeks. Thirdly, 80 percent of the members joined a local college on base to start preparing for their future. This was just short-term results that caused people to act on their faith and do something about their current life.

Now this program has been proven and mastered to present it to Christian leaders that are ready to grow the kingdom, build their businesses, excel in their current career, drive their financial capital, and most importantly build strong families. Having strong Big Goals will allow your life to change for the better. While reading this book you will see stories, quotes, scriptures, and other instructions to help you drive your life with Christ.

There is a story that really helped me find the mindset of some Christians today,

A city is experiencing a terrible flood. A man is sitting on his front porch watching the water rise and a jeep drives up. "Get in! Everything's going to be underwater!" "No thanks. God will save me. An hour passes and the water has risen in the house. A boat comes by. "Get in! You're going to drown!" "No thanks. God will save me." The water rises over the house. The man is now on the roof. A helicopter flies overhead. "We'll lower a line. Grab it or you'll die!" "No thanks. God will save me." The man drowns. When he gets to Heaven and meets God he says, "God! Why didn't you save me?!""I sent a jeep, a boat, and a helicopter. What more did you want?"

You don't have to be like the man in this story, take the help from this book, so your question to God won't be, Lord why didn't you save me? Allow this book to become a guide that will help push you into your destiny.

"Life can be pulled by goals just as surely as it can be pushed by drives."

-Viktor Frank

1

The Ability to Do!

"But someone will say, "You have faith and I have works." Show me your faith apart from your works, and I will show you my faith by my works." (James 2: 18 ESV)

....

"The safest principle through life, instead of reforming others, is to set about perfecting yourself."

-B. R. Haydon

THE PARABLE OF THE PIPELINE
a transformational story by Burke Hedges

Once upon a time long, long ago, two ambitious young cousins named Pablo and Bruno lived side by side in a small Italian village. The young men were best buddies, and big dreamers. They would talk endlessly about how someday, someway, they would become the richest men in the village. They were both bright and hard working. All they needed was an opportunity.

One day that opportunity arrived. The village decided to hire two men to carry water from a nearby river to a cistern in the town square. The job went to Pablo and Bruno. Each man grabbed two buckets and headed to the river. By the end of the day, they had filled the town cistern to the brim. The village elder paid them one penny for each bucket of water.

"This is our dream come true!" shouted Bruno. "I can't believe our good fortune."

But Pablo wasn't so sure. His back ached and his hands were blistered from carrying the heavy buckets. He dreaded getting up and going to work the next morning. He vowed to think of a better way to get the water from the river to the village.

Pablo the Pipeline Man

"Bruno, I have a plan," Pablo said the next morning as they grabbed their buckets and headed for the river. "Instead of lugging buckets back and forth for pennies a day, let's build a pipeline from the village to the river."

Bruno stopped dead in his tracks. "A pipeline! Whoever heard of such a thing?" Bruno shouted. "We've got a great job, Pablo. I can carry 100 buckets a day. At a penny a bucket that's a dollar a day! I'm rich! By the end of the week, I can buy a new pair of shoes. By the end of the month a cow. By the end of six months I can buy a new hut. We have the best job in town. We have weekends off and two weeks paid vacation every year. We're set for life! Get out of here with your pipeline."

But Pablo was not easily discouraged. He patiently explained the pipeline plan to his best friend. Pablo would work part of the day carrying buckets, and part of the day and weekends building his pipeline. He knew it would be hard work digging a ditch in the rocky soil. Because he was paid by the bucket he knew his income would drop. He also knew it might take a year or two before his pipeline would pay off. But Pablo believed in his dream and he went to work.

Bruno and the rest of the villagers began mocking Pablo, calling him "Pablo the Pipeline Man." Bruno, who was earning almost twice the money as Pablo, flaunted his new purchases. He bought a donkey outfitted with a new leather saddle, which he kept parked outside his new two-story hut. He bought flashy clothes and fancy meals at the inn. The villagers called him Mr. Bruno, and they cheered when he bought rounds at the tavern and laughed loudly at his jokes.

Small Actions Equal Big Results

While Bruno lay in his hammock on evenings and weekends, Pablo kept digging his pipeline. The first few months Pablo didn't have much to show for his efforts. The work was hard, even harder than Bruno's because Pablo was working evenings and weekends too. But Pablo kept reminding himself that tomorrow's dreams are built on today's sacrifices. Day by day he dug, inch by inch. Inches turned into one foot... then ten feet... then 20... then 100. "Short-term pain equals long-term gain," he reminded himself as he stumbled into his hut after another exhausting day's work. "In time my reward will exceed my efforts," he thought. "Keep your eyes on the prize," he kept thinking as he drifted off to sleep with the sounds of laughter from the village tavern in the background.

The Tables Are Turned

Days turned into months. One day Pablo realized his pipeline was half-way finished, which meant he only had to walk half as far to fill his buckets! Pablo used the extra time to work on his pipeline. During his rest breaks, Pablo watched his old friend Bruno lug buckets. Bruno's shoulders were more stooped than ever. He was hunched in pain, his steps slowed by the daily grind. Bruno was angry and sullen, resenting the fact that he was doomed to carry buckets, day in, day out, for the rest of his life.

He began to spend less time in his hammock and more time in the tavern. When the tavern's patrons saw Bruno coming they'd whisper, "Here comes Bruno the Bucket Man," and they giggle when the town drunk mimicked Bruno's stooped posture and shuffling gait. Bruno didn't buy rounds or tell jokes anymore, preferring to sit alone in a dark corner surrounded by empty bottles.

Finally Pablo's big day arrived, his pipeline was complete! The villagers crowded around as the water gushed from the pipeline into the village cistern! Now that the village had a steady supply of fresh water, people from around the countryside moved into the village and the village prospered.

Once the pipeline was complete, Pablo didn't have to carry buckets anymore. The water flowed whether he worked or not. It flowed while he ate. It flowed while he slept. It flowed on weekends while he played. The more the water flowed into the village, the more money flowed into Pablo's pockets!

Pablo the Pipeline Man became known as Pablo the Miracle Maker. But Pablo understood what he did wasn't a miracle. It was merely the first stage of a big, big dream. You see, Pablo had bigger plans. Pablo planned on building pipelines all over the world!

Recruiting His Friend To Help

The pipeline drove "Bruno The Bucket Man" out of business, and it pained Pablo to see his old friend begging for drinks at the tavern. So, Pablo arranged a meeting with his old friend.

"Bruno, I've come here to ask you for your help." Bruno straightened his stooped shoulders, and his dark eyes narrowed to a squint. "Don't mock me," Bruno hissed.

"I haven't come here to gloat," said Pablo. "I've come here to offer you a great business opportunity. It took me more than two years before my first pipeline was complete. But I've learned a lot during those two years. I know what tools to use now, and where to dig. I know where to lay the pipe. I kept notes as I went along so now I have a **system** that will allow me to build another pipeline in less time... then another... then another. I could build a pipeline a year by myself, but what I plan on doing is teach you how to build a pipeline, and then have you teach others and have them teach others.

"Just think, we could make a small percentage of every gallon of water that goes through those pipelines." Bruno finally saw the big picture. They shook hands and hugged like old friends.

Pipeline Dreams In A Bucket-Carrying World

Years passed. Their world pipelines were pumping millions of dollars into their bank accounts. Sometimes on their trips through the countryside, Pablo and Bruno would pass villagers from other villages carrying buckets. The friends would pull over and tell them their story and offer to help them build a pipeline. But sadly, most bucket carriers would hastily dismiss the notion.

"I don't have the time."
"My friend told me he knew a friend who's uncle's best friend tried to build a pipeline and failed."
"Only the ones who get in early make money on a pipeline."
"I've carried buckets my whole life, I'll stick to what I know."
"I know people who lost money in a pipeline scam."

Both men resigned themselves to the fact they lived in a world with a bucket-carrying mentality... and only a very small percentage of people would ever see the vision.

Turn Your Buckets Into Pipeline

What I love most about this story is that Pablo had a vision even while taking buckets of water into the village. Success starts first by doing something about your dream. It's so amazing that Pablo could have a vision to produce something even with no money, knowledge, or resources. Buckets should only be a part of your process to get you to being able to build a strategy for your dream.

As leaders our life should be built around our actions along with our faith. James told us in the verse listed about for us to show him faith without works and he will show you faith with his works. You have to go through your bucket experience with a pipeline vision.

Growing up I use to hear preachers say that "…If we take one step, God will take two" I've never found this in the Bible, but I believe if you take one step the path for other steps will appear. Just like when a baby takes their first steps, they start off shaky, and then end up more confident. Take a step of action towards your future.

How To Measure Success

Ask yourself these questions:

1. Personal Success Who am I? Do I possess Character? Do I have a good relationship with God? Am I a person of Integrity?

2. A Successful Family Am I Respected?- How is my relationship with my family? Do those who know me best respect me most?

3. Vocational Success Am I a successful businessman? Am I fulfilling my vocational or entrepreneurial call by using my gifts, leading by example and empowering others to do the same?

4. A Successful Ministry-Am I serving others? Do I love others as I love myself?

5. SUCCESS IN LIFE- Am I fulfilling Gods calling and purpose for my Life? Do I love God with all my heart, my mind, my soul, and all my strength?

Here are 10 Ways not to determine success:

1. Your bank balance.

2. How fancy your car is.

3. How fancy your house is.

4. How fancy your clothes are.

5. The shape of your body.

6. How other people see you.

7. How popular you are.

8. What school you attended.

9. Your family name.

10. Your position or status.

Success is when you feel happy about what you're doing, and what you do pleases God or has integrity.

Notes

Next Steps

Start thinking about how your life can change with hard work and dedication. Write down the biggest obstacle that could stop you from reaching your goals?

_____

_____

Now write down what your bucket is?

_____

_____

_____

Name three things that you can do to implement your pipeline system today:

1. _____

   _____

2. _____

   _____

3. _____

   _____

Now list three short-term goals that you would like to accomplish by the end of this book?

_____

2

Think Positive!

"For as he thinketh in his heart, so is he: Eat and drink, saith he to thee; but his heart is not with thee." (Proverbs 23:7 NKJV)

....

"A successful man is one who can lay a firm foundation with the bricks others have thrown at him."

David Brinkley

A story by By Francie Baltazar-Schwartz

Jerry was the kind of guy you love to hate. He was always in a good mood and always had something positive to say. When someone would ask him how he was doing, he would reply, "If I were any better, I would be twins!"

He was a unique manager because he had several waiters who had followed him around from restaurant to restaurant. The reason the waiters followed Jerry was because of his attitude. He was a natural motivator. If an employee was having a bad day, Jerry was they're telling the employee how to look on the positive side of the situation.

Seeing this style really made me curious, so one day I went up to Jerry and asked him, "I don't get it! You can't be a positive person all of the time. How do you do it?" Jerry replied, "Each morning I wake up and say to myself, Jerry, you have two choices today. You can choose to be in a good mood or you can choose to be in a bad mood.' I choose to be in a good mood. Each time something bad happens, I can choose to be a victim or I can choose to learn from it. I choose to learn from it. Every time someone comes to me complaining, I can choose to accept their complaining or I can point out the positive side of life. I choose the positive side of life."

"Yeah, right, it's not that easy," I protested.

"Yes it is," Jerry said. "Life is all about choices. When you cut away all the junk, every situation is a choice. You choose how you react to situations. You choose how people will affect your mood. You choose to be in a good mood or bad mood. The bottom line: It's your choice how you live life."

I reflected on what Jerry said. Soon thereafter, I left the restaurant industry to start my own business. We lost touch, but often thought about him when I made a choice about life instead of reacting to it. Several years later, I heard that Jerry did something you are never supposed to do in a restaurant business: he left the back door open one morning and was held up at gunpoint by three armed robbers. While trying to open the safe, his hand, shaking from nervousness, slipped off the combination. The robbers panicked and shot him. Luckily, Jerry was found relatively quickly and rushed to the local trauma center. After 18 hours of surgery and weeks of intensive care, Jerry was released from the hospital with fragments of the bullets still in his body. I saw Jerry about six months after the accident. When I asked him how he was, he replied, "If I were any better, I'd be twins. Wanna see my scars?"

I declined to see his wounds, but did ask him what had gone through his mind as the robbery took place. "The first thing that went through my mind was that I should have locked the back door," Jerry replied. "Then, as I lay on the floor, I remembered that I had two choices: I could choose to live, or I could choose to die. I chose to live."

"Weren't you scared? Did you lose consciousness?" I asked. Jerry continued, "The paramedics were great. They kept telling me I was going to be fine. But when they wheeled me into the emergency room and I saw the expressions on the faces of the doctors and nurses, I got really scared. In their eyes, I read, 'He's a dead man.' I knew I needed to take action."

"What did you do?" I asked.

"Well, there was a big, burly nurse shouting questions at me," said Jerry. "She asked if I was allergic to anything. 'Yes,' I replied. The doctors and nurses stopped working as they waited for my reply… I took a deep breath and yelled, 'Bullets!' Over their laughter, I told them, 'I am choosing to live. Operate on me as if I am alive, not dead."

Jerry lived thanks to the skill of his doctors, but also because of his amazing attitude. I learned from him that every day we have the choice to live fully. Attitude, after all, is everything.

Having the right attitude in leadership is very important for a leader when mapping out their lives. Your thoughts will manifest your outcome, which is why it is very important to look for positives and solutions in life instead of complaining. This lesson is geared to help you think positive and accomplish Big Goals.

The call to leadership is a very admiral desire and task, because it allows individuals that love Jesus to utilize their passions and gifts for the kingdom. Things that individuals normally do not look at when they take on the task as a leader are the costs. Leader in the Greek means "Chief Servant" this indicates that leadership cost for sacrifice, obedience, daily devotion, time management, and commitment.

The secret to a good leader from a bad leader is simply the attitude of the individual. We see this even out of the first

family in the Bible with Cain and his brother Able. God received Able's sacrifice because he had the right attitude verses his brother Cain who gave God His left overs.

God wants our best and deserves our best. In this lesson we would like for you to examine your heart to discover your recommitment to God in the matter of your attitude.

There are three key things that people looks for in a leader: Attitude, Aptitude, and Appearance.

1. **Attitude:** Manner, disposition, feeling, position, with regard to a person or thing.

2. **Aptitude:** Capability, ability, and innate or acquired capacity for something (Talent)

3. **Appearance:** The act or fact of appearing to the eye or mind before the public.

Leaders should have a balance of all three of these qualities. Out of all three of these qualities the attitude is the most important quality of all, simply because people judge us by our attitude.

The way that you think about yourself will always determine your outcome, so when lemons are thrown at you make lemonade, and when bricks are thrown at you build a brick house; you determine the outcome of your life.

Just like Jerry in the story, His attitude determined if he would live or die.

Notes

Next Steps

Start thinking about how you have used all three of these qualities: Attitude, Aptitude, and Appearance. Which is your weakest point?

_____

_____

Now write down which quality is your strength?

_____

_____

_____

Name three things that you can do to implement your these three qualities:

1. _____

   _____

2. _____

   _____

3. _____

   _____

What should we do when bricks are thrown at us?

_____

3

The Heart to Serve

*Do nothing from rivalry or conceit, but in humility count others
more significant than yourselves. Let each of you look not only
to his own interests, but also to the interests of others. Have
this mind among yourselves, which is yours in Christ Jesus,*
(Philippians 2: 3-5 ESV)

....

*"Defeat is not the worst of failures. Not to have tried is the true
failure"*

George Edward Woodberry

Five Qualities of a Servant's Heart

1. THE HEART OF A SERVANT IS HUMBLE – What is humility?
Humility is not denying your strengths. Humility is being honest
about your weaknesses. Humility is when you're so focused on
serving other people that you don't even think about yourself.
"All of you must put on the apron of humility to serve one
another. For God resists the proud but gives grace to the
humble." 1 Peter 5:5

2. THE HEART OF A SERVANT IS COMPASSIONATE AND
LOVING – Sympathy is when you say, 'I'm sorry you are hurt.'
Empathy is when you say, 'I hurt with you.' But compassion is
when you say 'I'll do anything I can to stop your hurt.' In
Matthew, chapter 9, the Bible says that Jesus was filled with

compassion.

3. THE HEART OF A SERVANT IS OBEDIENT – A servant obeys God, not out of convenience, but conviction. A lot of people want to serve the Lord if it's convenient, but a real servant will serve the Lord from conviction. "The one thing required of a servant is that he be faithful to his master." 1 Corinthians 4:2

4. THE HEART OF A SERVANT IS NOT SELFISH – A servant will put others before himself. He will relinquish his rights in order to serve others. It was once said that the true way to joy in our lives is Jesus first, Others second, You (ourselves) last. "Jesus gave up everything and became a slave when He became like one of us." Philippians 2:7

5. THE HEART OF A SERVANT ENCOURAGES OTHERS - A true leader will build up those around him. A true leader makes those around him better people with his words, actions and reactions. "Encourage and help each other, just as you are already doing." 1 Thessalonians 5:11

Serving others is very important; but remember, it starts at home.

Having the right heart is essentials for any one that really want to make an impact. Having a Mobilized Action Plan for your life will always be re-developed by those you have treated with love. Make a commitment to treat others rights. The golden rule tells us to do unto others, as you would want them to do unto you. Make that a core value in your life.

King David prayed and asked God to, "Create in me a clean heart, renew in me the right spirit..." God wants us to come heart first, full of love, and Jesus will be our guide.

How do we have a Servant's Heart? Jesus example:

- He Listens:
- He Offers No Excuses:
- He Is "On Mission":

III. How Do I Get There From Here?

1. Don't Get Hung Up On Past Failures

2. Pray. Watch. Listen. Then, Do.

Notes

_____

_____

_____

_____

_____

_____

_____

_____

_____

_____

_____

_____

_____

_____

_____

_____

_____

_____

Next Steps

Start thinking about how your heart and how you can make an impact simply by doing something. Write down how you plan to become more heartfelt?

_____

_____

Now write down what is on your heart to do?

_____

_____

_____

Name three things that you can do to implement the how to:

1. _____

   _____

2. _____

   _____

3. _____

   _____

List two ways that you go to help others:

_____

4

Stop Listening to Chickens!

Do not be unequally yoked together with unbelievers. For what fellowship has righteousness with lawlessness? And what communion has light with darkness? And what accord has Christ with Belial? Or what part has a believer with an unbeliever?

(2 Corinthians 6:14-15 NKJV)

....

"God grant me the serenity to accept the things I cannot change, the courage to change the things I can, and the wisdom to know the difference."

Reinhold Niebuhr

There was an eagle's nest that contained three large eggs. One day a bad storm rocked the eggs to tumble down to a chicken's farm. By instinct the chickens knew they must protect and care for the egg, so an old hen volunteered to nurture the large egg.

One day, the egg hatched and a beautiful eagle was born. But the eagle was raised to be a chicken. After a while the eagle believed he was nothing more than a chicken. The eagle loved his family and home, but just felt that there was more for him. While playing a game on the farm with his other chicken friends, the eagle looked in the sky and saw the eagles soaring. The eagle cried out, "I wish I could fly like those birds." The chicken laughed and said, "You cannot soar like those birds, you're a chicken we cannot soar." Finally the eagle died and remained a chicken.

The eagle shows four major leadership characteristics:

1) Vision - Just like the eagle, all leaders must have vision. The eagle's eyes can see great distances. They can also directly into the sun without being blinded. You, being the leader of your church team, must have vision. You must have a vision that guides and leads your team towards the organization's goals. The vision must be big and focused. A big, focused vision will produce big results.

2) Eagles Never Eat Dead Meat - You will never see an eagle eating meat that it did not kill. An eagle is not a scavenger. It hunts for and kills its own food. It hunts for the prey while it's warm and alive. You as a leader must go where the action is. You must go where hunt down and find lively people to grow you church or business.

3) Looks For & Flies Into Storms - As storms approach, lesser birds head for cover, but the mighty eagle spreads its wings and with a great cry mounts upon the powerful updrafts, soaring to heights of glory. Eagles use the storm to lift him to these great heights. Leaders use storms (challenges); we don't run from them. To leaders, storms are tools used for their development. The eagle's eyes can see great distances...you must have a vision that guides and leads your team.

4) Very Gentle & Attentive To Their Young - The eagle is known for its ferocity, yet no member of the bird family is more gentle and attentive to its young. At just the right time, the mother eagle begins to teach her eaglets how to fly. She gathers an eaglet onto her back, and spreading her wings, flies high. Suddenly she swoops out from under the eaglet and as it falls, it gradually learns what its   wings are for until the mother

catches it once again on her wings. The process is repeated. If the young is slow to learn or cowardly, she returns him to the nest, and begins to tear it apart, until there is nothing left for the eaglet to cling to. Then she nudges him off the cliff.

As a leader having an eagles approach will allow you to become a powerful focused leader that will help your church or business grow and go to new heights.

There is an eagle in you that is ready to fly into success and do the impossible. The one thing that you must do though is try to fly, so many of us dream about flying and reaching Big Goals but for some reason we listen to our environment, friends, and family members that normal make us feel that it's impossible.

Quit listening to negative people today, because you are unevenly yoked and stuck. It's so amazing that many people listen to people that is in the same situation that they are in.

• An eagle is a leader that can go through any situation or storm life throws their way and fly above it.

• An eagle is confident in its God to know that faith is real

• An eagle never gives up

Are you an eagle or a chicken? If you listen to chickens you will be like the eagle in this story that died with talent, strength, and power. I challenge you to find the eagle inside of you, because it's time to fly.

Notes

_____

_____

_____

_____

_____

_____

_____

_____

_____

_____

_____

_____

_____

_____

_____

_____

_____

_____

Next Steps

Can you relate to the eagle in the story? Write down how?

_____

_____

Now write down how not to be like the eagle in the story?

_____

_____

_____

Name three things that you can do to prevent yourself from dying like the eagle:

1. _____

_____

2. _____

_____

3. _____

_____

List two things that the eagle could of done to change his outcome:

_____

5

Clarify Your Vision!

"Where there is no vision, the people perish..."

Proverbs (29:18 KJV)

....

"Every man builds his world in his own image. He has the power to choose, but no power to escape the necessity of choice."

Ayn Rand

THE POWER OF VISION!

The ability to see beyond our present reality, to create, to invent what does not yet exist, to become what we not yet are. It gives us the capacity to live out of our imagination instead of our memory.

-- Steven Covey (1994, p103) First Things First

What is a Vision?

A vision begins as an idea in your imagination that you have a desire to make real. The idea turns into the intention and will to achieve that idea. Refining and clarifying the idea along with the intentions to achieve it are   what turn into the vision.

Defining your Vision?

- Creating a vision is a process of nurturing and cultivating ideas and imagination.
- Differentiate between the future that would become real and the future of your vision.
- The vision must be about changing that which is likely to occur, rather than changing that "which is".
- The vision is about changing the world in a way that wouldn't have normally happened.
- The vision must distinguish between what must change and what must not change. It must be clear and well-defined to be a real vision.

Questions you should ask yourself when planning your vision plan:

1. What were some challenges, difficulties and hardships you've overcome or are in the process of overcoming? How did you do it?
2. What causes do you strongly believe in? Connect with?
3. If you could get a message across to a large group of people. Who would those people be? What would your message be?
4. Given your talents, passions and values. How could you use these resources to serve, to help, to contribute? (to people, beings, causes, organization, environment, planet, etc.)
5. What makes you smile? (Activities, people, events, hobbies, projects, etc.)
6. What are your favorite things to do in the past? What about now?
7. What activities make you lose track of time?
8. What makes you feel great about yourself?
9. Who inspires you   most? (Anyone you

know or do not know. Family, friends, authors, artists, leaders, etc.) Which qualities inspire you, in each person?
10. What are you naturally good at? (Skills, abilities, gifts etc.)
11. What do people typically ask you for help in?
12. If you had to teach something, what would you teach?

Quotes to Remember:

"Vision without action is a daydream. Action without vision is a nightmare"

-Japanese Proverb

"Action may not always bring happiness:

but there is no happiness without action"

-Henry Van Dyke

"Our goals can only be reached through a vehicle of plan in which we must frequently believe, and upon which we must vigorously act. *There is no other road to success."***-Steven Brennan**

"Obstacles are those frightful things you see when you take your eyes off your goals." **-Unknown**

"Imagination is more important than knowledge"

-Albert Einstein

"It is better to aim high and miss then to never aim at all"

-Unknown

"Only those who attempt the absurd ... will achieve the impossible"

-Anonymous

"I always wanted to be somebody,but I see now I should have been more specific. " **-Lily Tomlin**

Notes

Next Steps

What is your vision? Write it in one sentence.

_____

_____

Now why is this vision?

_____

_____

_____

Name three things that currently prevent you from accomplishing your vision:

1. _____

_____

2. _____

_____

3. _____

_____

Now write one thing that you are going to do differently:

_____

_____

"You cannot dream yourself into a character; you must hammer and forge yourself one."
Henry David Thoreau

6

Principles of Communication!

"Where there is no vision, the people perish..."

Proverbs (29:18 KJV)

....

"Every man builds his world in his own image. He has the power to choose, but no power to escape the necessity of choice."

Ayn Rand

God is the Great Communicator, and He has revealed many important communication principles in the Bible. By following these keys, and we can strengthen our relationships and learn to think and act more like our loving Creator.

Esther 7 tells the dramatic story of the conversation in which Queen Esther saved her people:

"So the king and Haman went to Queen Esther's banquet. And while they were drinking wine that day, the king again asked her, 'Tell me what you want, Queen Esther. What is your request? I will give it to you, even if it is half the kingdom!'

"And so Queen Esther replied, 'If Your Majesty is pleased with me and wants to grant my request, my petition is that my life and the lives of my people will be spared. For my people and I have been sold to those who   would kill, slaughter, and annihilate us. If we had only been sold as slaves, I could remain quiet, for that would have been a matter too trivial to warrant disturbing the king.'

"'Who would do such a thing?' King Xerxes demanded. 'Who would dare touch you?' "Esther replied, 'This wicked Haman is our enemy'" (Esther 7:1-6, New Living Translation).

What Keys to Good Communication Does the Bible Give?

What we say and how we listen to others is important to God. He warns us that "death and life are in the power of the tongue" and that we must give account of "every idle word" we speak (Proverbs 18:21; Matthew 12:36).

What summary principles for good communication and interpersonal relations did James record?

Communication Continued...

James 1:19So then, my beloved brethren, let every man be swift to hear, slow to speak, slow to wrath...

Many of the communication pitfalls that wreck relationships come from violating these three keys. We tend to be slow to listen but quick to speak our minds, and in the resulting confusion and selfishness we are very quick to get our feelings hurt and to get angry.

In this lesson we will focus on the first two points James made: being swift to hear and slow to speak.

Swift to HearWhat happens if we are quick to speak instead of quick to hear?

Proverbs 18:13He who answers a matter before he hears it, it is folly and shame to him.

It's natural to think we know   what other people want or

need before they finish asking. And we generally assume that what we have to say is what the other person should really be interested in hearing. Listening skills are rarely taught and generally neglected.

Next Step:

We have to overcome this lack of training by focusing on the other person and forcing ourselves to try to understand his or her viewpoint before sharing our own.

What mind-set must we avoid in order to truly understand another person? Proverbs 18:2

A fool has no delight in understanding, but in expressing his own heart. We all want to, and are taught to, express ourselves. But when our desire for self- expression keeps us from trying to really understand the other person, we are being foolish and selfish. This is the opposite of the attitude the apostle Paul encouraged: "Let nothing be done through selfish ambition or conceit, but in lowliness of mind let each esteem others better than himself. Let each of you look out not only for his own interests, but also for the interests of others" (Philippians 2:3-4).

Tips for improving our listening include:

•Smile and look the other person in the eye naturally (it's not a stare down).

•Ask questions to show you are interested and to clarify things you aren't sure of.

•Look for common ground.

•Try to block out distractions.

•Don't focus on rehearsing what you will say next.

•If the person expresses   strong feelings; try to

acknowledge them without becoming offended or angry yourself.

Key Example:

How did David ask God to help him with his communication?Psalm 141:3, New Living TranslationTake control of what I say, O Lord, and keep my lips sealed. Psalm 19:14, New Living Translation

May the words of my mouth and the thoughts of my heart be pleasing to you, O Lord, my rock and my redeemer.Obviously David didn't mean he wanted his lips permanently sewn shut. Though we can't keep our lips sealed at all times, we all want our words to be pleasing to God.

We can't get through life without communicating. In fact, Proverbs 10:19 clarifies that it is a "multitude of words" that generally causes the problem. We should avoid being overly talkative and garrulous. Also we must be very careful to think before we speak and to choose our words carefully. Whatever we say should be edifying and intended to reflect the nature of Christ and to glorify God.

Let's look at some of the keys God gives for good communication. Communication Continued...What should we choose to say?

Colossians 4:6Let your speech always be with grace, seasoned with salt, that you may know how you ought to answer each one.

Philippians 4:8Finally, brethren, whatever things are true, whatever things are noble, whatever things are just, whatever things are pure, whatever things are lovely, whatever things are of good report, if there is any virtue and if there is anything praiseworthy— meditate on these things.

"The essential thing is not knowledge, but character."
Joseph Le Conte

7

Get Out of The Pot with Crabs

"Be sober-minded; be watchful. Your adversary the devil prowls around like a roaring lion, seeking someone to devour." (1 Peter 5:8 ESV)

....

Goals are the fuel in the furnace of achievement.

-Brian Tracy, *Eat that Frog*

I can remember back to a story that I once heard that really made this topic come to life, "Here's the thing, he said, there will always be one crab that gets his claw up on the rim of that pot and is just about ready to pull himself out of there. And then the other crabs will grab him and drag him back into the pot. They're not getting out of there, but they're going to make sure he's not getting out either. Both of you guys are smart and talented. You could go places. Don't let them drag you back into that pot, boys."

Crabs In Your Life

There are some people in your life that don't want to see you succeed. These are those friends and family members that are negative and toxic. As a leader you have to surround yourself around people that are positive and want to see you accomplish your goals.

If you are the biggest crab in your pot it's time for you to search for another pot! This story is a true fact that crabs pull other crabs back down into the hot water as they scream.

Getting out of the Pot

Wreck The Routine!

How To Get Out Of The Pot: If you find yourself stuck in a cycle, immediately change your routine. Sit at someone else's desk if you work in an office. Sit outside if you work at home. Move away from the routine to restart your creativity. I like to go for a drive - I go out at lunch every day to force myself to "wreck the routine". It is too easy to get caught up doing the routine things - when what you should be doing is thinking outside the box on how to grow your business. Get up and move yourself to move your business. Keep moving until you no longer have a routine and then enjoy the business growth and new ideas you will be ready to implement!

Unlocking Your Mind

How To Get Out Of The Pot: Change your perspective + process your knowledge & experience = making the ordinary...extraordinary & the unusual...commonplace. Look at the same thing as everyone else and think something different.

Stockpile Ideas For The Lean Times

How To Get Out Of The Pot: When I get stuck in a rut I look for inspiration from individuals outside my field and also refer to my trusty "Not-Now-List". Many of my top ideas come when I am too overwhelmed to act on them. When things get slow I look to my list of ideas that I forgot I thought of long ago. Sometimes I even surprise myself and think "I thought of that?!". Doing this keeps me fresh and always looking to expand who I serve and keeps my approaches unique!

Keys To Creativity:

How To Get Out Of The Pot: If you're stuck...

Pick up a book, take a class, listen to a CD, but learn something new. Doesn't matter what it is, or whether it's connected to your field. Look for the unexpected connections.

Experiment and make mistakes. Explore. Try something unexpected. Take breaks. Stop and reflect on what you're doing. The eureka moment comes when least expected. Be patient. Getting out of the box takes time!

Start Every Day As If It Were The Last Day Before Vacation

How To Get Out Of The Pot: Think about the last time you packed up the car and headed for your favorite travel destination. The day before you left you had to organize your clothes and possibly those of others to fit neatly in a cramped space. You had to make a list and stock up on food and items you'd need while away. You had to pay your bills and take care of things that would happen in your absence such as canceling the mail or newspaper delivery. Think of what you'd accomplish if you experienced everyday with the same strategy, vigor and follow through as the day before you left for vacation.

Notes

Next Steps

Can you relate to the eagle in the story? Write down how?

_____

_____

Now write down how not to be like the eagle in the story?

_____

_____

_____

Name three things that you can do to prevent yourself from dying like the eagle:

1. _____

_____

2. _____

_____

3. _____

_____

List two things the eagle could of done to change his outcome:

_____

_____

8

Never Give Up!

"But someone will say, "You have faith and I have works."
Show me your faith apart from your works, and I will show you
my faith by my works." (James 2: 18 ESV)

....

*Thomas Edison dreamed of a lamp that could be operated by
electricity, began where he stood to put his dream into action,
and despite more than ten thousand failures, he stood by that
dream until he made it a physical reality. Practical dreamers do
not quit.*

-Napoleon Hill

The secret to accomplishing Big Goals is simply never quit.
There were times in my life that I quit ever project when it got
bad. I would use the frame that if God wanted me to have it he
would make away. This is just a sorry excuse to justify you
being faithless. The first project I quit when it got too hard, I
lost out on a project that is now worth five million dollars. The
second project about two million dollars.

The issue that I had most with this two major successful
projects that I spent months on sky rocketed about two weeks
after I quit the first time and one month on the other one. I
thought that I had had luck, but I just had a bad case of
quitting.

Could you imagine being like Thomas Edison that had ten thousand failures, but still kept trying until his dream became a reality. You will never accomplish Big Goal quitting when things get hard. Things normally get worse before they get better you just have to hang in there.

Faith without works is dead according to the Bible, so in order for you to become a better leader, husband, wife, teenager, employee, business owner, pastor, alter worker, and usher you must Mobilize your Action Plan by setting realistic goals and sticking to them. So let's begin!

1. **Get a clear view of your Goals**
2. **Determine the Purpose of your Goals**
3. **Commit to your Goals publicly**
4. **Create a Action Plan**
5. **Review Goals regularly**

Steps to Accomplishing BIG GOALS!

• The more clarity the higher chance to accomplish it

• Visualize that you have already accomplished your goal

• Then start writing down what it feels like and look like

• What's at stake?

• How will make you feel?

• Does it benefit others?

• This will make you stay focused because others are watching you

• Give you support from   friends and family members

- Makes you accountable to yourself and others

- It has to be detailed

- Realistic

- Measured by Time (Short Term & Long Term)

- Reflect

- Revise

- Retry

Please on your notes pages start creating a rough draft of what this all looks like. It time to get into gear to see a major change in your life. Like start driving.

Notes

Next Steps

What was the largest goal you've accomplished?

_____

_____

What does winning feel like?

_____

_____

_____

Name three things that you can do to re create that feeling:

1. _____

   _____

2. _____

   _____

3. _____

   _____

List two actions that will help you get on track:

_____

_____

Learning is the beginning of wealth. Learning is the beginning of health. Learning is the beginning of spirituality. Searching and learning is where the miracle process all begins.

-Jim Rohn

MAP GOAL ACHIEVING SYSTEM

The MGAS is geared towards helping people master and discipline for becoming a successful Christian leader. MGAS is a fuel system for to help people drive their life, family, ministry, church, and business. For the next six weeks challenge yourself. Follow the simple exercises to achieve BIG GOALS!

5 BASIC STEPS TO GOAL PLANNING Your Steps to Success:

1. **Plan-** *be intentional with your daily functions*

2. **Prepare-** *think your day through*

3. **Evaluate-** *the positives and negatives of your daily functions*

4. **Act-Do** *something about your life plans*

5. **Rethink-** *learn from mistakes*

Q. How do you build a brick house? The answer to this is one brick at a time, this is the same when it comes to building our lives, build it one action at a time.

MAP GOAL ACHIEVING SYSTEM SUCCESS TRACKER (WEEKLY)

What Action steps are you taking to change your life?MGAS is only a tool that can help you reach your goals, you must work hard and be dedicated to changing and learning in order to become a master at accomplishing BIG GOALS.

Q. How do I get the most out of my goals? Goal are the most essential objectives in the life anyone that have vision. The only way to get the most out of your goals your work have to match. No one will ever get big results without putting it hard work.

Now it's time for you to get in the driver's seat and drive down a journey that is full of success!

SUCCESS WORKSHEET

(Dream Big)

I would like to achieve

_____

_____

I would like to donate

_____

_____

I would like to help

_____

_____

I would like to study

_____

_____

I would like to live in

_____

_____

I would like to drive

_____

_____

I would like to own

_____

_____

I would like to travel to

_____

_____

I would like to (anything else)

_____

(Shape Your Attitude)

Having a positive outlook on life is important
because_____

_____

I'll work on having more self-discipline by

_____

_____

To gain confidence, I'll have to

_____

_____

I'll need to be assertive, therefore

_____

_____

To stay focused, I'll need to

_____

_____

To achieve my goals, I'll need to

_____

_____

I'll learn to cope with failure by

_____

_____

(Discover Your Passion)

If I had all the time and money in the world, then right now I'd
be

_____

My three favorite activities are

_____

_____

I enjoy spending my free time on

_____

_____

I'm a very knowledgeable person when it comes to

_____

_____

(Create Opportunities)

Can you remember any new inventions you thought about at one time but never followed through with? If so list it here.

_____

_____

Have you ever written any plays, poems, novels, music, etc. that you have never published? List it here.

_____

_____

Have you ever thought of a way to improve an existing invention, but never followed through with it? List it here

_____

_____

Do you think you have a natural talent for something? In other words you know you are really good at it, without even trying. If so list here.

_____
_____

Is there an existing type of business out there that you are
really interested in? Maybe one day have a similar one? If so
list here.

_____

_____

_____

_____

_____

Quotes for Success:

"Be your character what it will, it will be known, and nobody will take it upon your word."
Lord Chesterfield

"Reputation is what men and women think of us; character is what God and angels know of us."
Thomas Paine

"Nothing of character is really permanent but virtue and personal worth."
Daniel Webster

"It requires less character to discover the faults of others, than to tolerate them."
J. Petit Senn

"A good name will shine forever."
Proverbs

Daily Goals Checklist:

- Is it realistic?

- Who is already doing it?

- How does it fit into your monthly goals?

- How will you accomplishment?

- Who will hold you accountable?

- Personal Development (books read, self improvement workshops, etc.)

Monday-
Tuesday-
Wednesday-
Thursday-
Friday-

Give yourself a weekly progress report (1-5)

Monthly Goals Checklist:

Examine your overall score of daily goals from previous weeks. Look for areas of improvement and strengths.

Monthly Daily Scores:

1-5 (Below Average)
6-11 (Average)
12-16 (Achiever)
17-20 (Over Achiever)

* Note to see big results you must put in the work

Quarterly Goals Checklist:

Two months have to be Achiever to be going on the right track in this program. You must try to strive daily to accomplishing your goals.

Month One:

Month Two:

Month Three:

Also make sure that your provide a weekly review:

Week 1:

Week 2:

Week 3:

Week 4:

Week 5:

Week 6:

Week 7:

Week 8:

Week 9:

Week 10:

Week 11:

Week 12:

David Brown, Sr.
Founder of the Oneighty Leader

Following high school, David joined the U.S. Navy and fought in the Gold War. Afterwards joined the US Army where he became a Master Trainer and was awarded for being an inspiration to his peers and friends.

Drawing on skills honed as an educator, business owner, and speaker, David has created and conducted training programs for groups ranging from international corporations and trade associations to governmental agencies and educational institutions. His client list includes the VA Medical Center in San Diego, the Phoenix Children's Hospital, the Dream Center, the NBA, South University, University of Phoenix, the U.S. Army and a host of other international businesses and education-related organizations.

Now working as a motivational speaker, a leadership consultant, and owns multiple businesses. David notes that James Wright was the father he never had and has taught him business practices at the tender age of 18 while serving in the U.S. Navy.

David is CEO of the Oneighty Leader, a business meeting, training, and development the leadership needs of individuals, organizations and churches. He resides in San Diego, CA with his wonderful wife and their son David brown Jr.

"Action is the foundational key to all success"

-Pablo Picasso

www.ingramcontent.com/pod-product-compliance
Lightning Source LLC
Chambersburg PA
CBHW041623110426
42740CB00042BA/34